THE
Words I Couldn't Say To You

SARAH CHIRITA

authorHOUSE®

AuthorHouse™
1663 Liberty Drive
Bloomington, IN 47403
www.authorhouse.com
Phone: 1 (800) 839-8640

Published by AuthorHouse 12/17/2019

ISBN: 978-1-7283-3994-8 (sc)
ISBN: 978-1-7283-3995-5 (e)

Sarah Chirita, a Romanian-American, is an artist in multiple forms. Whether it be through poetry, music, or painting; she finds a way to express herself. Sarah hopes to help others find some healing through her words. She understands what it feels like to not always have the right words to express ourselves with. This is her debut poetry book "The Words I Couldn't Say to You." Which takes readers on a journey from heartbreak to self-love.

I love you.

I miss you.

Love was there in the way we looked at each other, In the way we laughed a little too hard at two pm and held one another a little too tight at two am. We saw right through one another... everyone saw our love, but you and I felt it.

*I love being your soft place
when life gets hard.*

Nothing can explain the feeling that washed over me the night you first told me you loved me, I waited four years to hear those three words and it only took two seconds for you to say it.

Our love was the loudest feeling and we could only ever fully feel it in the quietest of rooms, just us two.

I've memorized that look by now, just kiss me you fool.

We had the kind of passion that actors would practice for months to achieve, meanwhile we had it from the first moment we met.

That's the magic in love, it's different for everyone, so nobody but us will ever know what our love felt like.

You were the rhythm in my dance,
you were the muse for my paintings,
you were my lyrical inspiration,
you were the first poem I ever wrote,
I incorporated you into all the things I love,
because you too were yet
another thing I loved.

*I lost my voice, not literally, I just got
so lost, so broken, I couldn't muster
out a note, and then came you, and
I remembered why I fell in love with
singing in the first place, and you, you
not only made me realized why I loved
singing, but the music we made together
is why I will never lose my voice again.*

I always loved your brown eyes, your eyes were like the dock I caught a glimpse of while I was caught in the midst of the raging sea, I found refuge in them.

*I don't think you'll ever not
give me butterflies*

If someone gifted me a ticket
to go anywhere,
The only place I'd want to
go is in your arms.

I longed to photograph you in your happiest moments to show you that you've been happy before, even if but a split second, so you will be happy again.

If I could, I would have framed the way you looked at me, because it wasn't just a "look" you saw me, truly saw me. In a world where I thought I went unnoticed, there you were, noticing me.

You were the adventure I never got to take

I was in love with the man I thought you could be

Sometimes, your first love isn't always your forever love.

*I would start from the beginning
but all I can seem to remember
is all our various endings.*

You held onto me like you held onto everything, you didn't.

You hid behind your mask for so long that it had become permanently plastered onto you.

It's not love that you're afraid of... it's being loved back that absolutely terrifies you.

We were the definition of "opposites attract"
they do attract, but they also subtract.

You know it's truly agonizing that after everything, when you called needing something I still answered the phone with the same excitement as I always did, but when I called you that one night, you answered with "who is this?"

*Life has thrown boulders at me,
what you did was merely just a
pebble being flicked at me.*

*I guess that's what happens, that's
what always happens, right?
You're left there perfectly fine,
meanwhile all the women you hurt
are left there surrounded by their
brokenness, little do you know that their
brokenness is really their strength.
You need to know that when women share
a common factor like pain, they come
together to help one another and that,
that is where the revolution begins.*

*You've been running from things
your whole life, that's what
makes you love the chase.*

I told you about all the things people did to hurt me, I should have realized that all I was doing was giving you pointers on how to hurt me just like they did.

You completely reassembled me, no wonder everybody asked why I wasn't myself; I didn't know how to be unless you were there controlling me.

How could you just completely erase me from your memory like that? It was as if I was the rain falling on your windshield and you just wiped me away.

I don't remember what it felt like to hold your hand, I just remember the feeling of your fingertips on the edge of mine, because you were never holding on, you were always letting go.

I will have to spend forever with the memory of what almost was

You knew I would have waited forever for you, so that's why you let me go.

*You're not what I want anymore,
I think you stopped being what I
wanted when I found out about
you two. Seriously? In my bed?*

You think you know what's best for me?
Well you don't, because if you did then you
never would have hurt me in the first place.

How is it that you can restore my faith in love and also destroy it at the same time?

I tried, but take tried and rearrange the letters, you get tired. I got tired of being the only one who tried.

What did it feel like? What did it feel like to break my heart? I know it wasn't your first time, although you seemed to enjoy breaking mine the most because you kept doing it over and over again.

I wanted to be held, not kept, you didn't know the difference.

*You were the person who was
most afraid to hurt me
which is ironic since you were
the one to destroy me.*

I got so lost in you, and that's where I lost myself.

You were lonely, not because you wanted me, rather because you had absolutely no idea who you were, you were lost in yourself, and that is one of the darkest and loneliest things in this world, to not know who you are in a world where everybody pretends to know.

Love is quite simple, you made it arduous

I wonder if things would have worked if we met four years from now...

Maybe you weren't my forever,
You were my hope that someday I'd find it.

*I shouldn't have to teach you
how to love me correctly.*

Pain surrounded me but I managed to escape it, only to run into its arms all over again when I met you.

*You don't even care to listen, so
I don't even care to speak*

Your inability to love me gave me the capability to finally love myself. Thank you.

Goodbye.
We said that many times,
This time I really mean it.
No, that's not a lie.
And if we happen to bump into each
other again just know that I still love
you, but we will never be more than
ex's who just remained "best friends."
At least that's the last thing you
said to me before I left.

Now I have already dedicated fifty pages to you, so the next fifty are the words I couldn't say to myself. You taught me more about love with heartbreak, than you ever did with anything else. I kept it short and simple because that's how our relationship was (minus the simple part, of course.) I know you hate reading, so I didn't want to be a bore. These first fifty pages hold the past five years with you and the next fifty are for me, and the fifty after that, and after that, and after that will be pages you'll have never touched, and that is both heartbreaking, yet, satisfying at the same time. I love you, I told you the day before I left that twenty years from now, I'll still love you, because love doesn't go away. True love. Your first love. It never does, if it does, it was never love in the first place. So, thank you for being my first real love and my longest heartbreak. You reminded me who I am, and to fall in love with the amazing woman I have always been, it just took me a little while to realize it. Thank you, here's to you, to us, and now onto me. This is me quite literally closing the chapter on us.

The Words I Couldn't Say to Myself

- *First off, I feel like I just lost so*
much weight since the last page.
Not literal weight, metaphorical,
but either way, it's weight.
If only I would have told you sooner,
Your worth isn't in how much you weigh.
It's in the way you pray your prayers.
The way you fall asleep and wake
in a mini puddle of drool.
The way you feel.
The way you laugh.
The way you forgive.
The way you love.
When you think of weight, don't think
of gym weights or body weight. Think
of how you've had the weight of the
world on your shoulders for so long and
you've handled it in the best way you
could. I'm proud of you. I love you.

I'm sorry I put you through situations that could have been prevented.

I forgive you.

I'm proud of you.

You are seen.

Your existence matters.

*Give yourself the patience
that you never received*

*You are a masterpiece working
on mastering peace.*

You handled the pain like poetry.

Just as you fall, you will also rise.

Those years' worth of tears brought you here, they watered the soil that you stand on now, remember that.

Take the help, it doesn't make you weak, it means you just need a moment to breathe.

You are not the things that broke you, you are all the pieces coming back together

*You have carried this pain long
enough, it's time to set it down.*

You are not that scared little girl again.

You can't go back to the girl you were before; you can be better; you can finally unleash the woman who has been eagerly waiting to come out.

*You are a good woman and you don't
have to convince a good man of that
because he will already know.*

Once you realize that you don't need them, that's when you can finally stop wanting them

If it's continuously crossing your mind, you've already decided.

You have to be the one who breaks the cycle.

*By being strong you're building a
bridge from your past to your future.*

When it's all falling apart hold
onto yourself even more.

*Darling, the love you were searching
for was inside you all along.*

You have your whole life to fall in love with yourself, start now.

You are not your parents.

If all you could do today was breathe then you've done more than enough.

Going through the brokenness will soon make you whole again

Think of it like this, a flower is closed off and then as time passes and the seasons change it slowly but surely begins to open up and bloom, it blooms for a period of time and then the petals fall and it's a whole cycle that repeats itself but the point is that it WILL bloom again. So, remember that, you're in this closed off, dark, lonely place but you will bloom again into the lightness and love of this life and it will be beautiful. You will bloom again; it just takes time.

This will be the story you will tell your kids when they feel like giving up.

You are like the Earth, the Earth restores and replenishes itself, parts of it are eroded while other parts are growing. You may feel like you're broken in one aspect but in the other you are being renewed.

You can't prevent certain things from happening, learn to accept what each season brings.

You don't owe anyone an explanation
on the way you chose to heal.

Your past self is proud, your current self is waiting, and your future self is excited to meet you.

This is all just character development.

You never know how you're going to make it, but you always do and that is your power.

Believe in something, anything. Believe in yourself, that's always a good place to start.

Accept the compliment, even if you don't believe it, accept it, let it in and it'll plant that first seed of confidence.

I craved this perfect, story book love, I forgot that there already is a perfect, storybook love written for me, it's called The Bible.

You learn truth in temptation

You are not a bad person for saying "no."

Beauty begins when reality sets in

Love yourself so much that you make others want to love themselves too.

You are your home, get cozy.

Healing is all you have after someone destroys you.

Your love is something sacred,
spread it wisely.

All those prayers you thought went unanswered, here they are now, answered.

Maybe, just maybe, you were placed in their life for this exact moment.

The light isn't at the end of the tunnel,
it's inside of you, you just need to turn
it on to help you find your way out.

*Your worth was never found on Earth,
it was always known in Heaven*

You made it - God

Printed in the United States
By Bookmasters